CAPRICORN

CAPRICORN

23 December–20 January

PATTY GREENALL & CAT JAVOR

MQP

Published by MQ Publications Limited
12 The Ivories
6–8 Northampton Street
London N1 2HY
Tel: 020 7359 2244
Fax: 020 7359 1616
Email: mail@mqpublications.com
www.mqpublications.com

Copyright © MQ Publications Limited 2004
Text copyright © Patty Greenall & Cat Javor 2004

Illustrations: Gerry Baptist

ISBN: 1-84072-764-0

1 3 5 7 9 0 8 6 4 2

Printed in Italy

WHAT IS **ASTROLOGY**?

Astrology is the practice of interpreting the positions and movements of celestial bodies with regard to what they can tell us about life on Earth. In particular it is the study of the cycles of the Sun, Moon, and the planets of our solar system, and their journeys through the twelve signs of the zodiac— Aries, Taurus, Gemini, Cancer, Leo, Virgo, Libra, Scorpio, Sagittarius, Capricorn, Aquarius, and Pisces — all of which provide astrologers with a rich diversity of symbolic information and meaning.

Astrology has been labeled a science, an occult magical practice, a religion, and an art, yet it cannot be confined by any one of these descriptions. Perhaps the best way to describe it is as an evolving tradition.

Throughout the world, for as far back as history can inform us, people have been looking up at the skies and attaching stories and meanings to what they see there. Neolithic peoples in Europe built huge stone structures such as Stonehenge in southern England in order to plot the cycles of the Sun and Moon, cycles that were so important to a fledgling agricultural society. There are star-lore traditions in the ancient cultures of India, China, South America, and Africa, and among the indigenous people of Australia. The ancient Egyptians plotted the rising of the star Sirius, which marked the annual flooding of the Nile, and in ancient Babylon, astronomer-priests would perform astral divination in the service of their king and country.

Since its early beginnings, astrology has grown, changed, and diversified into a huge body of knowledge that has been added to by many learned men and women throughout history. It has continued to evolve and become richer and more informative, despite periods when it went out of favor because of religious, scientific, and political beliefs.

Offering us a deeper knowledge of ourselves, a profound insight into what motivates, inspires, and, in some cases, hinders, our ability to be truly our authentic selves, astrology equips us better to make the choices and decisions that confront us daily. It is a wonderful tool, which can be applied to daily life and our understanding of the world around us.

The horoscope—or birth chart—is the primary tool of the astrologer and the position of the Sun, Moon, Mercury, Venus, Mars, Jupiter, Saturn,

Uranus, Neptune, and Pluto at the moment a person was born are all considered when one is drawn up. Each planet has its own domain, affinities, and energetic signature, and the aspects or relationships they form to each other when plotted on the horoscope reveal a fascinating array of information. The birth, or Sun, sign is the sign of the zodiac that the Sun was passing through at the time of birth. The energetic signature of the Sun is concerned with a person's sense of uniqueness and self-esteem. To be a vital and creative individual is a fundamental need, and a person's Sun sign represents how that need most happily manifests in that person. This is one of the most important factors taken into account by astrologers. Each of the twelve Sun signs has a myriad of ways in which it can express its core meaning. The more a person learns about their individual Sun sign, the more they can express their own unique identity.

ZODIAC WHEEL

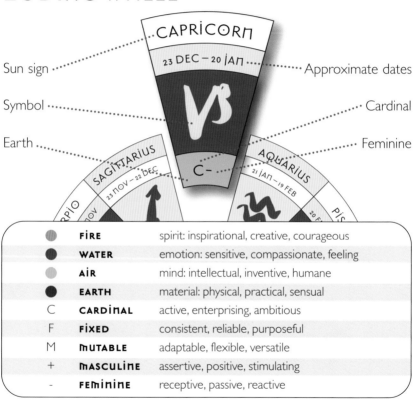

Sun sign .... Approximate dates

Symbol .... Cardinal

Earth .... Feminine

CAPRICORN

23 DEC – 20 JAN

SAGITTARIUS

23 NOV – 22 DEC

AQUARIUS

21 JAN – 19 FEB

C–

🔴	**FIRE**		spirit: inspirational, creative, courageous
⚫	**WATER**		emotion: sensitive, compassionate, feeling
⚪	**AIR**		mind: intellectual, inventive, humane
⚫	**EARTH**		material: physical, practical, sensual
C	**CARDINAL**		active, enterprising, ambitious
F	**FIXED**		consistent, reliable, purposeful
M	**MUTABLE**		adaptable, flexible, versatile
+	**MASCULINE**		assertive, positive, stimulating
–	**FEMININE**		receptive, passive, reactive

ARIES
21 MAR – 20 APR

TAURUS
21 APR – 21 MAY

GEMINI
22 MAY – 21 JUN

CANCER
22 JUN – 22 JUL

LEO
23 JUL – 22 AUG

VIRGO
23 AUG – 22 SEP

LIBRA
23 SEP – 23 OCT

SCORPIO
24 OCT – 22 NOV

SAGITTARIUS
23 NOV – 22 DEC

CAPRICORN
23 DEC – 20 JAN

AQUARIUS
21 JAN – 19 FEB

PISCES
20 FEB – 20 MAR

PART ONE

THE **ESSENTIAL** CAPRICORN

RULERSHİPS

Capricorn is the tenth sign of the zodiac and the third Earth sign after Taurus and Virgo. It is ruled by the planet Saturn and the symbols for Capricorn are the Mountain Goat and the mythological Sea Goat. There are earthly correspondences of everything in life for each of the Sun signs. The parts of the human body that Capricorn represents are the knees, bones, and skin. Capricorn is also a Cardinal and Feminine sign. Gemstones for Capricorn are dark green tourmaline, onyx, obsidian, jet, and smoky quartz. Capricorn signifies barren fields, places where sheep and cows are kept, and thorny places. It also represents bones and boundaries, chiropractors, contractors, masons, mathematicians, mayors, government officials, politicians, and osteopaths as well as rock salt, pine trees, hemlock, henbane, ice, time, watches, and clocks.

CAPRICORN

The parts of the human body that Capricorn represents are the knees, bones, and skin.

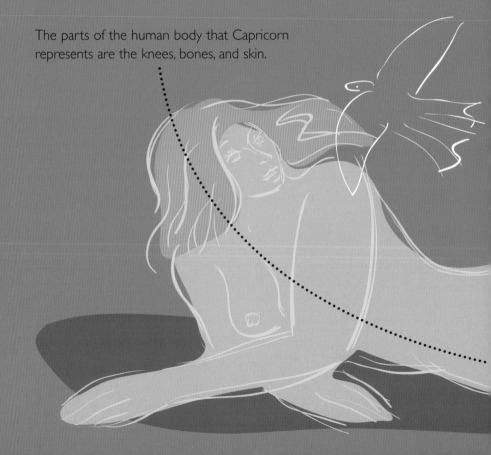

time, watches, and clocks

government officials, politicians, mayors

pine trees

PERSONALITY

It's not easy to enter into the world according to Capricorn let alone understand it once inside. On the whole, Capricorns are prudent and trustworthy, industrious, hardworking, and loyal. As they climb to the peak of their achievements they are sure-footed, like their symbol, the Mountain Goat. They are cautious and reserved yet they aren't afraid to take action when necessary. They also have a reputation for being a little dull and gloomy, but once people become more intimate with them, they discover that this is far from the truth. Capricorn is probably the most stable and serious sign of the zodiac and its natives possess enormous self-control. They are people to admire and rely on.

One of the most entertaining and endearing aspects of Capricorns is their great sense of humor, but it's not the type of humor that suits the fainthearted for it involves looking at the deepest, darkest chasms of experience and seeing the funny side of them. Capricorns don't turn a blind eye to the tragedies of life but instead embrace them and somehow manage to see the absurdity in them. They can often make a roomful of people laugh with their cynical quips about how ridiculous the human condition can be. Yes, their sense of humor is dark and full of irony and satire, but that's their way of dealing with life's inevitable pitfalls. And, by easing the transition between misfortune and laughter, their dark sense of humor is actually therapeutic.

However, the transition between misfortune and laughter doesn't happen immediately. Far from it. In fact, no one more than a Capricorn knows that time is a great healer, for Saturn, Capricorn's planetary ruler, is also known as Kronos, the Father of Time. Capricorn understands that it's only over time that we can see what's important in life and this understanding helps us to honor the temporal nature of our life on earth.

Being ruled by Saturn is also an indication of a certain heaviness and intensity. Somehow with Capricorns, that permeates their family, work environment, and their social group, but they are totally unconscious of this effect.

Capricorns are complex individuals, full of paradoxes yet consistent. The motivated, serious, self-controlled Capricorn is a very impressive person indeed, capable of achieving anything for themselves or for those they love. They are incredibly skilled at manipulating the material world and, as a result, at acquiring possessions and status. Their taskmasters in this endeavor are gritty reality combined with the application of practical understanding, so it is not surprising that Capricorns develop tenacity, determination, and patience along the path to fulfilling their aspirations. They are usually very aspirational people, always with a goal in mind for, without one—whether it be material, ideological, emotional, or spiritual—Capricorns would be lost, wandering through life without purpose, and easily depressed.

Although they are action-oriented people, bursting with powerful, tightly coiled inner energy, they are also thoughtful and contemplative, always taking a good look before they leap. Once they have their well-laid-out plan in front of them, it's not easy to divert them from it. They will put up with all sorts of difficulties and problems along the way, and will endure both minor and major disappointments if they see some deeper meaning and a higher purpose to their actions. They also like to feel that every expenditure of their immense energy has a purpose and a good chance of success, so they'll check and recheck their plans for any endeavor they're about to undertake. And this helps to explain why Capricorns are often considered traditionalists, since traditions are built up over time and have a solid grounding in the collective mind of society.

Being a valued and admired member of society is important to Capricorns; they put a lot of thought and hard work into attaining a high level of respect. If they are to become figures of authority, whether in their own field or in the broader context of society, for instance in politics and government, they must first adhere to society's rules and regulations. Capricorns like rules because they feel that these make life easier. Although adhering to them can be burdensome to others, they give practical Capricorns a structure upon which, by using their talents, they can build a higher superstructure. They can sometimes be social climbers, but for them that's not simply about being seen in the right company—although that has definite advantages.

Capricorns are often kind toward and considerate of those with whom they develop personal, nonwork-related relationships. However, it's a different story when it comes to those with whom they compete on the career ladder. They're not the type to use underhand methods to push competitors out of the way or to trample all over them on their way to the top; instead they simply ignore them—unless there's a possibility that working with them can further their own personal ambitions.

Capricorns have a hearty respect for those who have done well; they congratulate them on their efforts rather than feel envy, and they are continually inspired by being in close proximity to other people's success. Conversations with important, admired, or talented individuals are vital to Capricorns as such conversations often provide them with the tried-and-true knowledge and understanding that those people have gained on their path to success. In return, Capricorns have much to teach others about how to make the most of their potential and how to succeed in the world. But even those Capricorns who don't pursue success have a quiet dignity and demonstrate a hard-earned wisdom that it's impossible not to be impressed by.

CAREER & MONEY

It's rare to find a Capricorn who is out of work; if they are, it's only a short, transitory period in their lives while they find their true self again. They have a strong work ethic and are ambitious, but they're also aware of the fact that the best route to success is through determined effort. Since Capricorns are realistic and grounded, it would be quite unlike them to while away their time in fantasy. Instead, they use their time wisely, carefully contemplating their next move and making sure that they take the right steps, for they are very conscientious about their every action.

When they are young, Capricorns learn the virtue of patience and persistence in the face of what are sometimes great obstacles, and this sets them up perfectly with the strong spirit that they use in later life to tackle projects. That is when they are able to put to use all they have learned. It may take them a while to get where they are going, but Capricorns usually achieve success while other, less tenacious types, fall by the wayside. But Capricorns won't just trample over those who have fallen in the hope of being the first to achieve glory! They have a strong moral sense, particularly where work is concerned, and if they need to cover for someone else's mistakes rather than see a company's reputation besmirched, then they'll do so.

There are many occupations that suit Capricorns, for instance banker, financier, builder, architect, and engineer. They also have a great talent for government and politics. In fact, any career that allows them to climb the ladder of success to a position within the establishment will suit their talents and skills perfectly. The more mystical Capricorn is often attracted to the world of entertainment, particularly the music industry, or to occult or spiritual paths, such as the Church or New Age businesses. Capricorns want to change the world for the betterment of everyone, but particularly for themselves.

When it comes to money, Capricorn is rarely without, but Capricorns are resourceful so even if they're broke, they'll find a way to sustain themselves. However, if their pocketbooks are swelling, they won't be found boasting about it or flashing their cash, for excessiveness and extravagance are unknown to them. They may sometimes indulge but are more likely to treat themselves and a loved one to one of the simple pleasures of life—a great back rub, going to look at a magnificent view, or enjoying a walk in the countryside. If they are seriously rich—and many Capricorns are—they'll still live within their means.

Career and money are two areas of life that Capricorn will surely get a firm handle on, for they are practical, ambitious, and have a natural desire to better themselves. It's particularly in their early thirties that they really come into their own, start to consistently gather the fruits of their labors, and begin to blossom.

THE CAPRICORN **CHILD**

From the moment Capricorn babies are born they have a serious look on their face; after all, life is a serious business. Structure is very important to their sense of security, so having a strict routine of when to eat or sleep, when it's time for bath or for play, makes them much happier. Erratic timetables can make them grumpy or, when they're older, will make them act superior and tell Mom and Pop off for not delivering what's expected at the appropriate time. Young Capricorns also require physical contact and outward signs of affection so, if they're allowed, just as soon as they can get themselves out of the crib they'll regularly climb into their parents' bed for a cuddle.

They're respectful children and seem older than their years in their speech and mannerisms. Young Capricorns seem in a rush to grow up and have a tendency to emulate the behavior of their parents. Indeed, they frequently prefer the company of adults to that of other children; such behavior is often mistaken for clinginess and a lack of confidence to leave the parent's side. Because of this, they should be encouraged to indulge in childish games and to develop relationships with other children. The toys they prefer are those that offer a sense of purpose; they like building blocks, musical instruments, electronic games with increasing levels of difficulty, and collecting cards or figurines that go on sale on a regular day of the week or month. As the day comes around, the little Capricorn will be there, pocket money in hand, telling his or her parents that the next edition is available for purchase.

As Capricorn children grow into adolescence, they demonstrate self-discipline and a determination to do well at school, along with a high degree of common sense that means parents rarely have to worry about them when they're out with friends. But they could find the confusing emotions that come at this stage of development particularly difficult, and that can cause the Capricorn adolescent to withdraw behind a barrier of self-control and strictness that makes it hard for others to know what they're really feeling. At all stages of their life, the Capricorn child is a wise soul. They surprise people with the degree of maturity that they possess and their strong, interesting character makes them a pleasure to have around.

PERFECT GiFTS

Everyone loves receiving presents because it says something about how special they are to other people. Capricorns, too, enjoy opening a personally chosen gift, but the fact is that they are more impressed by a well-thought-out present wrapped in brown paper than by a lavish gift—unless they can exchange it for the cash! So if you're going for expensive or lavish, it would perhaps be better to simply give them a gift certificate or the money.

However, Capricorns aren't so difficult to buy for as long as a few pointers are kept in mind. Firstly, they tend to like heavy objects, preferably made of stone, so a sculpture for the home or garden would be ideal, or a desk accessory made of stone or wood. And as Capricorn is a sign that's very much linked to time, gifts such as watches, clocks, calendars, diaries, or journals to mark events and celebrations are always welcome.

It's always difficult to buy a more personal gift, such as clothing, but since Capricorn rules the knees, bones, and skin, Capricorns would appreciate something to keep them warm, such as an overcoat, a sweater, or a scarf. They'll definitely use it and will appreciate the fact that it was thoughtfully chosen.

FAVORITE **FOODS**

Capricorns are often accused of having hollow legs, because they can eat as much as any Taurus or Cancer but they rarely show any sign of where they put it. They seem to burn their food up before it even hits their stomach. Capricorns don't usually eat for comfort, but out of necessity, to provide them with the enormous amounts of energy that they expend in daily life. They aren't terribly adventurous with their food and prefer simple dishes to those with complex flavors, particularly when they're young. But neither are they overly fussy; they will sit down to eat what everyone else is eating. Eventually, over time, they build up a varied repertoire of favorite dishes.

Once they've passed their youthful growth spurts, they don't often snack between meals but prefer to keep to a regular timetable. For breakfast, fruit juice and tea or coffee alongside a serving of cereal and a round of toast give them the slow-burning carbohydrates they need to set them up for the first part of the day. However, for their midday meal they will usually choose something more substantial such as protein in the form of meat, fish, or cheese. Come the evening, they'll want to sit down to a traditional hot meal with all the trimmings. Though they aren't known for their sweet tooth, they are also likely to appreciate some form of pudding or dessert after their evening meal.

FASHION & STYLE

Capricorn is often a very dignified-looking clotheshorse, preferring an understated, unfussy, conservative style that combines quality and good taste, but they do have a tendency to hang onto favorite items of clothing long past the time when these looked their best. Luckily, because they usually choose classic, well-made outfits, even though they might get a bit shabby, they won't look like a relic of some trendy fad. Capricorns always like being attired appropriately for the occasion and they will rarely be under- or overdressed. If they don't have something to wear that suits the purpose, that will be the incentive for going off to the clothes stores, since for them, shopping for clothes is a necessity rather than a pleasure. They'll usually have planned out in their minds exactly what they're after before they go looking for it. They'll know which reputable designers and outlets to go to although they won't concern themselves with hunting down the latest in cutting-edge style.

They can wear most colors, whether bright, light, or dark and although a male Capricorn looks his most powerful and dignified best in a traditional dark suit with white shirt, and a female looks most sexy in a little black dress, they prefer not to wear moody, broody, dark colors all the time. If they wear patterned fabrics at all, they will probably keep them to an absolute minimum. Their shoes and accessories will be simple and stylish.

IDEAL HOMES

Capricorns have a good eye for style. The Capricorn home is earthy, practical, with a tendency toward minimalism, and perhaps a little on the dark side. They prefer darker colors such as brown, gray, bottle green, and beige, possibly so that more colorful objects will stand out in contrast.

When it comes to possessions, they own exactly what they need, no more and no less. They are organized and their homes are well-ordered, with everything in its place; no one need fear opening a closet in case chaos and confusion spring forth! This home has areas of uncluttered open space. Capricorns like to have practical storage in their homes. They won't object if anyone wants to go looking for skeletons in the closet; they have them, like most people, but theirs are only put away, not hidden away!

Those who prefer a comfy, cozy, warm dwelling, might feel that the Capricorn home is a little uninviting, but all they have to do is ask for the heating to be turned up or for the curtains to be closed. Capricorns spend much of their time at work so a little help from their friends to warm up their pad would be most welcome!

PART TWO

RISING SIGNS

WHAT IS A RISING SIGN?

Your rising sign is the zodiacal sign that could be seen rising on the eastern horizon at the time and place of your birth. Each sign takes about two and a half hours to rise — approximately one degree every four minutes. Because it is so fast moving, the rising sign represents a very personal part of the horoscope, so even if two people were born on the same day and year as one another, their different rising signs will make them very different people.

It is easier to understand the rising sign when the entire birth chart is seen as a circular map of the heavens. Imagine the rising sign — or ascendant — at the eastern point of the circle. Opposite is where the Sun sets — the descendant. The top of the chart is the part of the sky that is above, where the Sun reaches at midday, and the bottom of the chart is below, where the Sun would be at midnight. These four points divide the circle, or birth chart, into four. Those quadrants are then each divided into three, making a total of twelve, known as houses, each of which represents a certain aspect of life. Your rising sign corresponds to the first house and establishes which sign of the zodiac occupied each of the other eleven houses when you were born.

All of which makes people astrologically different from one another; not all Capricorns are alike! The rising sign generally indicates what a person looks like. For instance, people with Leo, the sign of kings, rising, probably walk with a noble air and find that people often treat them like royalty. Those that have Pisces rising frequently have soft and sensitive looks and they might find that people are forever pouring their hearts out to them.

The rising sign is a very important part of the entire birth chart and should be considered in combination with the Sun sign and all the other planets!

THE RISING SIGNS FOR CAPRICORN

To work out your rising sign, you need to know your exact time of birth— if hospital records aren't available, try asking your family and friends. Now turn to the charts on pages 38–43. There are three charts, covering New York, Sydney, and London, all set to Greenwich Mean Time. Choose the correct chart for your place of birth and, if necessary, add or subtract the number of hours difference from GMT (for example, Sydney is approximately ten hours ahead, so you need to subtract ten hours from your time of birth). Then use a ruler to carefully find the point where your GMT time of birth meets your date of birth—this point indicates your rising sign.

CAPRICORN WITH ARIES RISING

As energetic, upward movers, Capricorns with Aries rising make lots of forward leaps in life and yet manage to look where they're going before each and every one of them. Only the earliest of risers could catch them out, especially when it comes to work and career. They don't waste any time, so, to other people, they sometimes appear to make rash decisions. However, they don't; they have far too much common sense ingrained in them to do anything foolish. With their earnest determination and dogged perseverance, they get what they want out of life and have sufficient reserves of energy to outlast all other people. They may face disappointment as they try to reach the top, but they never lose their enthusiasm or ambition along the way. However, if they're thwarted in their efforts to be successful or to make an impact on the world, their fighting spirit can transform itself into an explosive, though usually quite short-lived, temper. These Capricorns often have an open, smiling face and are frequently the first to extend the hand of friendship and introduce themselves to new acquaintances. They are also quite eager to get to know everyone's business though they're not the prying type. They like everything to be aboveboard and they always take people at face value.

CAPRICORN WITH **TAURUS** RISING

These Capricorns have a double dose of determination and devotion; they aim high, work hard, and are rock-steady as they climb the ladder of success. Whether their goal is related to career, home, relationship, or something else, they'll throw themselves into achieving it with adamant resolve. It's like a formula for them; they work out their plan and then they put it into action. These Capricorns are often referred to as cool and calculating, which gives the impression that they are unfeeling, but this couldn't be farther from the truth for they have deep, passionate feelings; it's just their way of going about their business step by step, gradually getting closer and closer to their objective. They are very calm, quiet, kind people, who long to enjoy a serene life surrounded by expensive luxuries. They would rather do without than compromise on quality. However, when they are given the opportunity to indulge in hedonistic pleasure, they could certainly teach people a thing or two about the traditional delights of a bygone age for they are as extravagant in their lust for sensual excess as any emperor of ancient Rome.

CAPRICORN WITH **GEMINI** RISING

Compared with most Capricorns, the ones with Gemini rising are something of a chatterbox, but it's never quite certain whether their incessant chatter is a cover for something such as fearfulness or, perhaps, even for some hidden agenda. They'll be thinking about the "hows" and "what ifs" at the very same moment that they're talking in endless strings of well-constructed sentences. They have a natural talent for figuring out what's going on in other people's minds and are able to read between the lines of what others are saying. Good-natured and likable just the same, they have quite a penchant for communication, their acute sixth sense giving them the ability to cut to the chase and move fast intellectually. They'll still ponder things though, as all Capricorns like to do when they're alone, but Capricorns with Gemini rising are more instinctive, without really knowing quite how or why. They don't like discussing themselves, however, so should anyone try to push past their barriers and pry into their closely guarded secrets, they'll deflect them simply by changing the subject. And since there are so many subjects that are of interest to their deep, inquiring minds, they appear to others like intellectual giants with a wicked, witty sense of fun.

CAPRICORN WiTH **CANCER** RisinG

Sensitive and sincere, Capricorns with Cancer rising are people who go out of their way to be with others, work with others, and form almost any sort of alliance, but preferably on a one-to-one basis. They are loyal and dutiful, almost to a fault, and will be a friend for life, even when the other person chooses to walk away. They connect with others on the level of feelings, tending to get emotionally involved even in affairs of business, though not in any way that may compromise other areas of their life. It's simply that they care about those with whom they become involved. They are also builders of dynasties and are very devoted to their family, particularly the family they create with a marriage partner. They will put a lot of effort into having a happy home life and a successful working life and they enjoy the benefits that spring from these. These people often have quite an artistic flair; even if they don't use it in their career it can usually be seen reflected in their tastefully decorated, comfortable homes. They like nothing better than to be surrounded by their nearest and dearest in their very own space; here they can sit back, soak up the love, and repay it tenfold.

CAPRICORN WITH **LEO** RISING

Capricorns with Leo rising like to see themselves in the limelight and are willing to work their fingers to the bone to get there. It may not be the limelight of stage and screen, but it will be that of their chosen area of life. Whatever they do, they want to be seen, admired, and applauded for it. Yet they can also be shy when all the attention is turned upon them; they find it hard to strike a balance between wanting attention yet not wanting so much that it upsets their dry, sober disposition. However, because they always look as if they're in charge, they do naturally attract attention. For them, attracting attention isn't just about show; there has to be something solid beneath their glittering reputation. They may take their time trying out a few different career paths before finding where their true talents lie and before perfecting their skills in one specialized field. And while they can be nitpickers and can do the dramatic overreacting number better than any Hollywood ham, especially when they don't get their way, they're also warm, generous, and always willing to offer a shoulder to cry on when it's needed.

CAPRICORN WITH **VIRGO** RISING

There's a creative genius lurking beneath the surface of this fussy, exacting, subtle individual. These Capricorns are extremely practical people who can solve any everyday problem using means that are entirely obvious to them but are totally perplexing to others. Naturally helpful and earnest, they have a talent for explaining concepts and for interpreting and deciphering puzzles. This gives them a knack for unraveling the most complicated knots and putting everything back in order so that other, more simple, folk can get a grip on things that otherwise would have bamboozled them. They tend to be softly spoken and a little shy, however, and they don't seem to have a powerful sense of their own ego, but this can be deceptive because beneath that humble exterior lies a will of steel. Patient and practical, they'll make their way quietly to the top. They won't rock the boat for others but neither will they allow their own well-laid plans to be capsized. Far from being uncontrollable party animals, they do enjoy socializing and having a bit of fun, as well as entertaining others, so they're good value to have around. As a result, their social diaries are often full.

CAPRICORN WITH **LIBRA** RISING

The Capricorn with Libra rising is a joy to be around. They are pleasant and charming and have an ability to bring things together. They have always played the role of family mediator—and it wasn't always a comfortable role—and now it's as if they're expected to play it for life. However, it's not one that they can keep playing for long. After all, Capricorns are Capricorns; they're not usually friendly and all smiles, but if being so can bring about a favorable outcome, then they will be. These are very refined people with impeccable taste in clothes and traditional, old-fashioned manners. They often look as if they've stepped out of a magazine from a bygone era, when elegant sophistication and style were things to aspire to. Once they've found their niche in society, they stick with it, but because they're rather sociable it's probable that they'll hang out with a few different crowds, each with different interests. This Capricorn has very creative, lofty ideals as well as the practical know-how to make them into reality. They might start small, but may end up making a very big impact.

CAPRICORN WITH **SCORPIO** RISING

Perhaps the most penetrating and intuitive of all Capricorns, those with Scorpio rising possess an almost x-ray perceptiveness. They have a "dark" appearance even if they are of a light complexion. They seem to know what other people are thinking and have an excellent ability to put others' thoughts into words. They may not speak much but what they do say demonstrates their broad understanding of people and concepts. They are rather brainy, and it's when they put their thoughts on paper that their superior intellect has a chance to shine. They are self-contained, enormously self-controlled, and extremely guarded as to their personal feelings. They give very little away about themselves and maintain a commanding presence; there's absolutely no question of them exposing any sort of vulnerability. They run their lives with almost military precision and see any incursion into their privacy as enemy action, which can make them seem stern and uptight. They rarely lose their temper, but their retorts are sharp and wounding. However, they can also be sensitive, witty, and surprisingly lighthearted.

CAPRICORN WITH **SAGITTARIUS** RISING

For these Capricorns, what they own almost acts as a gauge for how they feel about themselves. The more they have to show for their hard work, the more secure they feel but, as they grow older, they become more relaxed about material success, usually because by then they've achieved the standard of living they expect and feel at ease with. Then it's not clear whether the comfort comes first or the relaxation, but either way, the two seem to go hand in hand. Sagittarius rising bestows a doubly wicked, satirical sense of humor on them, to which other people's reaction may be anything from a guffaw to indignant horror. These individuals can make light of even the most hideous aspects of life that other people usually prefer to ignore. They're capable of this because they're realistic and philosophical about the ups and downs of existence; they embrace all experience and view it all as valuable. For them, if one part of life is sacred, then it's all sacred; the only alternative is to think that nothing is sacred. Controlled and dignified as any other Capricorn, they often appear warmer and more exuberant. They are soulful people, full of wise words and ideas, and make good gurus.

CAPRICORN WITH **CAPRICORN** RISING

Penetrating, persevering, and serious, yet with a great sense of humor, the Capricorn with Capricorn rising is switched on and a delight to be with. These individuals are thoughtful and deep, with a strong sense of what's right and wrong. As a result, they usually go through life with an inner confidence and certainty. They don't like being told what to do because they feel that they already know! No matter how much they respect authority, they resist bowing to it absolutely. They have a no-nonsense approach to life and their exacting demeanor is one indication that they make few mistakes. Others will often turn to them for advice and to benefit from their wisdom. They'll frequently find themselves in a position of command because they're so good at showing others the way. Active and energetic in carrying out their duties, they're also very ambitious; however, they have a tendency toward overcautiousness, never setting their sights higher than what is immediately achievable. Failure, for them, would undermine their self-esteem so, rather than take risks in order to showcase their talents, they prefer to play safe.

CAPRICORN WITH **AQUARIUS** RISING

Unusually, this is a very idealistic Capricorn. These individuals have vast imaginations and possess a multifaceted inner world that can work in ways that help other people. With their artistic flair and their gift for tuning into the needs of others, they possess a healing ability. If harnessed and channeled properly, their talents could do wonders for their careers and their public standing—always major concerns for Capricorns. However, their imagination sometimes distracts them from pursuing their goals or fools them into believing that they have more resources than they actually do. For example, they may be encouraged to spend money like there's no tomorrow and then the usual Capricorn common sense vanishes. They are terribly sweet, if a little too eager to please; they could end up sacrificing both time and energy in their effort to be accommodating. These Capricorns don't mind occasionally kicking up their heels and breaking the rules, but they may suffer keenly from guilt if their behavior in any way upsets someone else.

CAPRICORN WITH **PISCES** RISING

Involvement with large groups is often the means by which these individuals choose to express their inner selves. Although Capricorn is rather reserved and can be rigid, Pisces rising softens the effect. The result is a more open, gentle, and easygoing nature that makes it easy for them to meld into the whole. Yet while they are part of the group, their individuality is always obvious; their hard work and persistent efforts help to make a real difference to projects that require team spirit. They are valued friends and members of society and they enjoy being in the company of interesting, creative, and unusual people. They possess these qualities in abundance but sometimes lack the confidence to show them unless they have a strong support network. Compassionate and caring, they can also be rather shy so they generally wait to be invited before regaling others with their quiet, dry wit. Once they're in full swing, though, these Capricorns feel like a gift from heaven to those around them. They are often rather musical, and through music they can employ their creativity and flow harmoniously with others. A musical hobby or career might provide them with much pleasure.

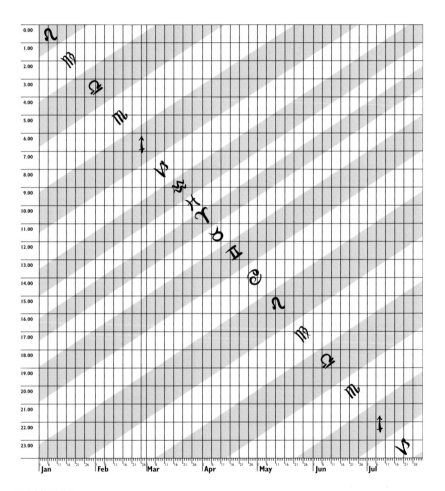

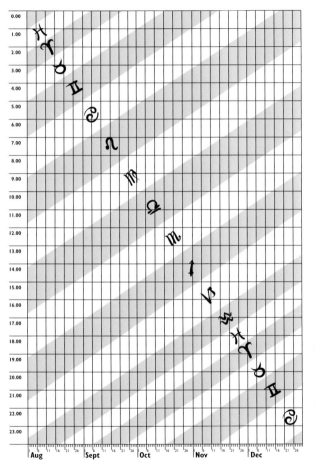

RISING SIGN
CHART

New York
latitude 39N00
meridian 75W00

♈ aries	♎ libra
♉ taurus	♏ scorpio
♊ gemini	♐ sagittarius
♋ cancer	♑ capricorn
♌ leo	♒ aquarius
♍ virgo	♓ pisces

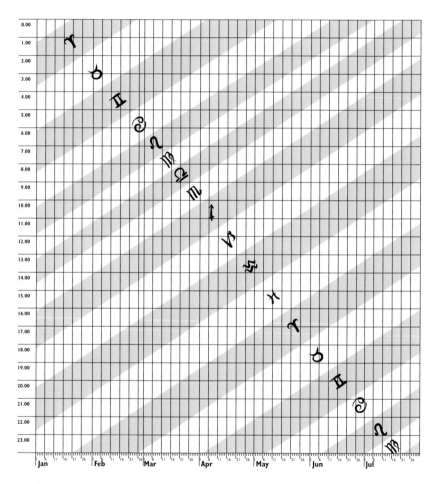

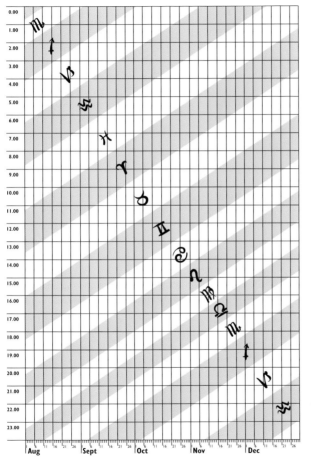

RiSinG SiGn
CHART

Sydney

latitude 34S00
meridian 150E00

♈ aries	♎ libra
♉ taurus	♏ scorpio
♊ gemini	♐ sagittarius
♋ cancer	♑ capricorn
♌ leo	♒ aquarius
♍ virgo	♓ pisces

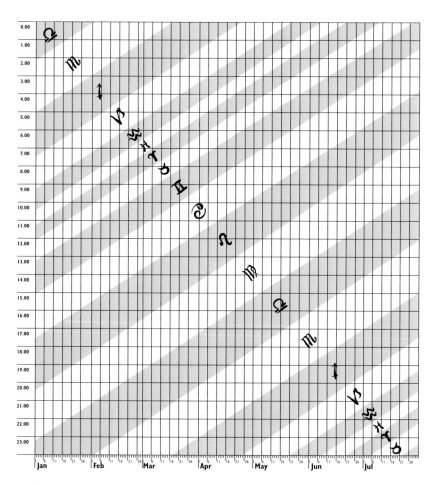

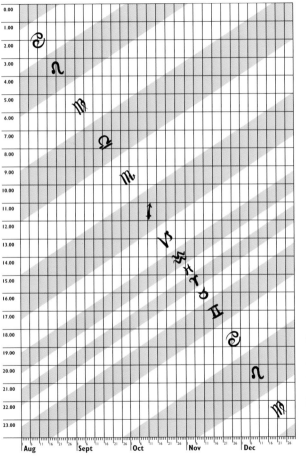

RISING SIGN
CHART

London

latitude 51N30
meridian 0W00

♈ aries   ♎ libra

♉ taurus   ♏ scorpio

♊ gemini   ♐ sagittarius

♋ cancer   ♑ capricorn

♌ leo   ♒ aquarius

♍ virgo   ♓ pisces

PART THREE

RELATIONSHIPS

THE CAPRICORN **FRIEND**

Although trustworthy and honest, Capricorn friends are usually very self-contained and prefer not to give too much of themselves away. Capricorns build relationships steadily and like to get to know people over time and through repeated exposure at social gatherings. Only then will they extend the hand of friendship unless, of course, they have a very good reason for wishing to make a connection sooner, for example if the person in question could assist them in their career or in achieving a better social standing. Then Capricorns are capable of going on such a charm offensive that those who know them well would be pleasantly surprised and would wish that they saw them more often. Once Capricorns have made a friend then they usually remain friends for life, whether regular contact is maintained or years go by with no contact at all. That's because Capricorns are rather choosy and require their friends to be interesting, entertaining, or deep thinkers with whom they can share "quality time." They enjoy a good party, though, and do occasionally indulge in lighthearted fun. They also have a marvelous sense of the ridiculous and can be extremely amusing when they're showing off their ironic sense of humor. But it would take quite a few drinks before they could let down their guard enough to be called the life and soul of the party. As time will tell, Capricorns are great friends and they are worth hanging on to.

CAPRICORN WITH **ARIES**

There's something unmistakable in the atmosphere when Capricorn and Aries meet but maybe it's not really desirable to have a Ram and a Mountain Goat charging at one another! They both want to be leader, which could create problems, so they each need to curb their self-centeredness in order to get along. Capricorns need to loosen up their apprehensive, even pessimistic tendencies, while Arians need to stabilize their impulsive, headstrong dispositions. There is a sense of excitement when they're together, as if something really big is about to happen, and more often than not, something very special does.

CAPRICORN WITH **TAURUS**

These two Earth signs have so much in common and so much they can do together. Both are grounded types of people, who can help, encourage, and advise one another, whether it's on the subject of making a sound investment or tackling some home decorating. They make the perfect pair and friendship will readily blossom between them. However, they sometimes feel that the outside world infringes on the time that they want to spend together, so they run the risk of shutting everyone else out. Both are realists, which leaves little room for imaginative horseplay, but who cares? As long as the chores are finished, all that's left to do is unwind and chill out!

CAPRICORN WITH GEMINI

Capricorn and Gemini frolicking down the street together and having a good time will look different at the start of their journey to when they finish. To begin with, they are all smiles and good intentions, though those intentions will differ. Later on, Gemini will be getting impatient waiting for Capricorn to catch up, while Capricorn will be feeling annoyed at being hurried and made to change pace—and then probably slow down deliberately. Capricorn's humor is a little dark for Gemini but, if they are prepared to give it a go, both could learn a lot from this friendship.

CAPRICORN WITH CANCER

Not all opposites get on as well together as Capricorn and Cancer. They are both ambitiously minded yet different enough not to actually clash in their aims. As friends, they can always rely on one another and their friendship could last a lifetime. Even when they live thousands of miles apart, they'll still stay in touch. A lot of the attraction is based on a shared sense of life's ironies, which afford them endless opportunities for wry amusement. They find it comforting to be with someone who totally understands how funny the paradoxes of life can be. This is a friendship that gets stronger the more one-on-one encounters they have.

CAPRICORN WiTH **LEO**

These two could form a mutual admiration society, but except for sharing a certain image-consciousness, they have absolutely nothing in common. Their differences lie in the way they approach life: Capricorn is careful, controlled, and contained, while Leo is wild, abandoned, and lavish, which makes them a rather odd combination. Strangely, this friendship can work if they respect one another and can see how their differences highlight their individual qualities. If they're on a mission together, they can count on one another to uphold their end of the deal and, eventually, they could very well find success.

CAPRICORN WiTH **ViRGO**

This is such an easy alliance—which is why Capricorn and Virgo become allies. Even on those rare occasions when they're not together, they're on each other's minds and should anyone have a harsh word to say about the other, they won't hesitate to stand up for them. These two will hang out together and will totally get where the other is coming from. In fact, with both of them so industrious, this friendship could probably develop into a creative partnership where they reap real material rewards as well as having fun together.

CAPRICORN WITH **LIBRA**

This is an energetic friendship that is constantly searching for an experience of intense connection, not only between themselves, but between them and the world that they encounter through their socializing. There can be an element of healthy competition, which helps both of them to reach farther and wider in their careers. But their friendship isn't always so serious; they're always up for a party and sharing a thrilling experience helps to bring these two together. Afterward, during the post-mortem analysis that they always indulge in, is when they find their sense of accord.

CAPRICORN WITH **SCORPIO**

These two make firm friends. They not only have a lot to say to each other, but they're honestly intrigued by and respond to the other's take on things. While they respect each other's personal boundaries, it's still possible for both of them to feel very relaxed and comfortable in each other's company. They don't feel any pressure to put on a performance because they agree about many things, such as what to do, where to go, or what to talk about. They simply meld and get along as if they were always meant to be together.

CAPRICORN WITH **SAGITTARIUS**

These two could be very good friends, particularly if they have a joint project that they both want to see completed. They'll inevitably find themselves joining forces on some issue or other because they get a real charge out of the way that their conversations start with nothing more than a good idea and end with the solid foundations of an excellent plan of action. Sagittarius helps Capricorn to see the lighter side of life, while Capricorn helps Sagittarius to take things a little more seriously, but they're not friends simply in order to be on a learning curve. They actually like each other and know that they're good for each other because what one lacks the other has, and vice versa.

CAPRICORN WITH **CAPRICORN**

When two Capricorns get together they maintain a quiet distance that is bridged by mutual respect and regard. They don't tread on each other's toes or get into conversations on highly emotive subjects; it's all very dignified and polite. Since there's little to find out about one another, they have the initial stages of friendship already sorted out, but what they can do is move forward and successfully build projects together. With their ironic appreciation of the ridiculous, if they're both in the mood, they can egg each other on and will quickly spiral into a state of backslapping hilarity.

CAPRICORN WITH **AQUARIUS**

This can be both a frustrating and a fulfilling friendship. Aquarius loves the challenge of shocking the almost unshockable Capricorn, while the solid Capricorn is inspired and intrigued by the rebellious, wacky ideas that magically emerge from the mind of Aquarius. They both enjoy getting locked into the dry, analytical conversations that sometimes ensue from their discussions of their lofty ideals. But where Capricorns are traditional in their views and actions, Aquarians are futuristic, avant-garde thinkers. Together, these two could either inspire one another by opening doors onto new vistas of thought, or they could extinguish one another's enthusiasm entirely.

CAPRICORN WITH **PISCES**

What a fertile friendship this can be! Somehow neither is put off by, but rather enjoys, the differences between them, namely imaginative, emotional idealism versus sound, practical reality. Pisces' no-holds-barred approach encourages Capricorn to let go of the sense of responsibility that can stop them from having fun, while Capricorn provides the type of solid camaraderie that doesn't drift away. Between them, one thing leads to another—Pisces will come up with ideas and Capricorn will help to make them concrete. They work in tandem in order to create a wonderful reality for themselves and for those around them. It's all so much fun that time just flies by when these two are together.

THE **CAPRICORN WOMAN** IN LOVE

This is not the type of woman to flutter her eyelashes, fall about in a romantic swoon, and hyperventilate because the hero of her heart is close by. Indeed, it's never very easy to tell whether the Capricorn woman is in love at all, because she's so calm and even-tempered—at least on the surface. Underneath, though, there can be a layer of molten hot passion and fierce love but it's not in her nature to express any of it openly and freely.

Like most other people, the early stages of Lady Capricorn's relationships are full of excitement, hope, and mutual physical attraction. She's a closet romantic and she longs to be swept off her feet by a dashing, distinguished, charming man. But she's also a realist and will be unconsciously checking out his credentials and testing his character for partnership potential. The Capricorn woman is looking for a solid foundation upon which to build a lasting commitment. If one isn't immediately apparent, she won't necessarily back off but will work with what she's got, perhaps taking on a parental role and trying to nurture what she sees as his good points. She'll throw the weight of her experience and know-how into assisting him in attaining his goals and in managing their time together so she can share as many of his interests as possible. But all the while she'll hold back a portion of her heart, not trusting either him or herself enough to reveal the full intensity of the passionate love that she's capable of. This, of course, is a double-edged sword since it can lead to disappointment in love, a common theme in the early stages of romance for a Capricorn woman. Being unable to leap before she looks, to rush in where angels fear to tread, or to cross the strict boundaries that she sets herself means that, while she'll never appear a fool, she might also make it difficult for shortsighted men to see beyond her cool exterior and into her warm, giving heart.

However, once the Capricorn lady has found her man and the two of them have settled down into a life of committed partnership, she really begins to show her true worth. Then she can relax and reveal all the other wonderful layers of her character—the spiritual searcher, the creative comedienne, the earthy sex goddess. Few women are as capable as she of the sort of heartfelt devotion that manifests itself in very real terms—as an affectionate, ever-faithful, and supportive lover. And provided she receives enough of this in return and is treated with respect, she's not overly demanding or dependent; she's too honest to play the helpless female in order to get her way. She'll pull out all the stops and do everything in her power to help her man climb up his career ladder—probably while continuing to climb to the top of her own—so that together they can build a dynasty of permanence, style, and material wealth. If behind every great man there's a great woman, then behind the greatest of men there must have been a Capricorn woman.

CAPRICORN WOMAN WITH **ARIES MAN**

In love: Despite the Capricorn woman's usual reserve and patience in getting to know a prospective romantic partner, there's a sense of urgency about this relationship that's fired by a need to get together quickly. Aries and Capricorn are people of action and they will waste no time finding out if it's a "yes" or a "no." One minute they're meeting each other for the first time, and the next they're hastily ripping the clothes off each other's bodies in an attempt to understand the extraordinary attraction that they feel for one another. If this union is to last, they need to make a conscious choice to work toward the same aims and to do all they can to keep the channels of communication wide open. As they're both such busy people, they'll need to set aside time to meet. This relationship could prove to be a really amazing coalition, but while they both battle against their egos, it might be that someone else comes along and proves that life doesn't have to be quite so hard. The energy and compulsion to be together is certainly there, and will probably never die, but whether they will be able to make it work to their mutual benefit is another thing entirely. Both Aries and Capricorn are sincere individuals and they are capable of being truly dedicated people, but if they are not basically compatible, this relationship could end up being a painful one. Both do, however, have good instincts, so they should be able to know whether this partnership is for keeps or just for fun.

In bed: The Aries man's driving force is remarkable. Afterward, the Capricorn woman will be asking herself, "Did that really happen?" Then, with a wicked smile on her face, she'll be asking her amazing Aries man, "Can we please do that again? I kinda missed it the first time." Fast and furious, hot and hurried. Will these two ever slow down? If the Capricorn woman fancies a quickie because she's busy and running late for an appointment, the Aries man will give it to her every time, and as often as she likes. And she is very unlikely ever to refuse his advances simply because there is so much pleasure involved in being with this very horny man. When both are craving some pure, unadulterated pleasure, they'll always be there for one another. This is the kind of relationship that will be deep, meaningful, torrid, and sexy, or just plain old convenient. Either way, neither will lose out. On the contrary, both will gain something amazing from each and every sexual encounter. They'll both find it compelling and each will initiate the act as often as the other. If intimacy grows and love abounds, this could be a very workable match, but if the love turns stale, it could be more like hard work for both and they would be better off quitting while they're ahead.

CAPRICORN WOMAN WITH **TAURUS MAN**

In love: Love between a Capricorn woman and a Taurus man comes easy. It just feels so natural to be in one another's company. He has all the qualities that she admires and wants in a partner— a strong character, good taste, creativity, and downright desirability—just as she, with her cool head, practicality, and inspiring character, appeals to him from their first meeting. His sixth sense lets him know that hidden under her controlled exterior is an intensely passionate soul just waiting to be released by the romantic security he can provide. It would be easy for these two Earth signs to start their relationship by first striking up a friendship, and it would be obvious to both that there was something more intimate going on beneath the surface. But both prefer to take their time in getting to know their potential partners, finding out what makes them happy or sad, mad or glad. They don't trust flash-in-the-pan flirtations; they want to be sure that the infatuation is more than just a passing phase. Neither is willing to make a premature commitment but once they do decide to hand over their hearts, it will be for certain. So while they shouldn't expect fireworks from day one, they should feel the strange, low rumbling that warns them that the earth is about to move. This relationship just feels so right that they'll never be in any doubt that it's a match made in heaven. His love makes the Capricorn woman feel deeply secure.

 In bed: If the Capricorn woman ever wants to feel like a sex object—which actually happens all the time, though she'd never let on!—then the Taurus man can certainly oblige. She'll be his sex object, but one that is loved, adored, and respected all at the same time. Each of these highly physical people can find in the other someone who yearns for the sort of touch that cuts to the chase and doesn't waste hours on verbal foreplay that is clearly only a prelude to something else. They've already spent the time getting to know each other during the courting stage, and they will undoubtedly be constantly aware of the nearly tangible sexual tension that exists between them, so once they've made the decision to go for it, they go for it! In fact, it's possible for the Capricorn woman and Taurus man to do all their communicating without using any words. They have an unspoken agreement to abandon themselves to physical pleasure. It's as though each trusts the other to do all that's required to reach a climactic union. This relationship is so sexy that it would be amazing if they find time for anything else. If you could be a fly on the wall, it would be an incredible turn-on to see how their bodies are drawn together like powerful magnets, and cannot be separated until they have both reached a climax of incredible pleasure.

CAPRICORN WOMAN WiTH GEMINI MAN

In love: The Gemini man can bring out the playful side of the Capricorn woman, while the Capricorn woman can bring out a more stable side in the Gemini man. It's not often that she meets someone who can shake the heaviness out of her spirit, and it's just as rare that he meets someone who can make him feel so close to settling down. His light, happy sense of humor is highly infectious, and he appreciates it when she is able to put her intensity into words. Both have a need to laugh at the absurdity of life, and as long as the jokes keep coming, then they'll keep the relationship going. However, Gemini can sometimes appear too flaky for

Lady Capricorn's more practical approach to life; she knows the value of a good idea, but has little time for endless ingenuity unless she can see him putting it into action. He'll be impressed by her aspiring soul but gets impatient with her need to create a sturdy staircase to carry her upward when he can just sprout wings and fly. It doesn't seem to matter to him that he'll only ever make fleeting visits to the summit. Though she takes longer to get there, once she does she'll have a permanent place to stand, high above everyone else. In some way, these two make a perfect partnership. Each has something the other lacks and, deep down, they really do admire one another for it.

 **In bed:** The Gemini man is a chatterbox, in the bedroom as much as anywhere else, so the trick for the Capricorn woman is to stop him talking and get him touching! Although she appreciates his need to make a big mental "thing" about their lovemaking, and she will patiently indulge him, it can get a bit frustrating waiting around while he builds himself up. By the time he finally gets going, she'll be almost there but, as a Capricorn, she'll be able to pace herself. She's a very physical woman and she longs to feel him get up close and personal with her. She could certainly help him along by reading him some erotic poems or stories—and that's the perfect foreplay for a Gemini man who is filled with sexual fantasies. But he always likes to feel he has an escape route, which is why, even when all he wants to do is swoop down and dive on his Capricorn lover, he'll pretend that this is the last thing on his mind. When he does it, of course,

it will take her by surprise. But without the steady buildup she needs, it could all be over before she's halfway to the climax. This is where her ability to take charge and her firm grasp really come in handy. The only problem is that he finds this so intensely erotic that he might end up falling over the edge before she can catch him!

CAPRICORN WOMAN WITH **CANCER MAN**

 In love: In many ways, the Capricorn woman and Cancer man were made for each other. They have an instinct about each other and they understand each other totally, even before they've had a chance to have a heart to heart. The attraction between them is enormous and they have such similar intentions that they can get lost in each other completely, forgetting who said what or did what. The gentle, caring Cancer man makes the Capricorn lady go weak at the knees, and she has such a very special talent for building up his self-esteem that she makes him feel good about himself as no one else can. And why wouldn't she? He has that deep-rooted sensitivity and action-oriented quality that she so admires. When these two get together it feels as though the world has set itself to rights. They make a truly formidable team as they're both ambitious and they both feel happier when there's someone to share the fruits of their labor with. Many a night will pass with the two of them curled up on a comfortable sofa together, drinking fine wine from the family crystal, and congratulating each other on their successes. But there is a downside: the

Cancer man has a tendency toward frequent moodiness and if one of his dark moods coincides with one of hers, then it could all feel a little heavy around their place. Most of the time however, their realistic, stable, and heartwarming love just grows and grows.

In bed: These two are not as shy around one another as they can be with other Sun signs. When they're together they have the feeling that they can be totally themselves and they are uninhibited. Her passion is all tightly coiled intensity, while his is languorous and relaxed, so he'll push this way and she'll pull that way. Although it might seem as if they're coming at it from different perspectives, somehow it always works out in the end and satisfaction's guaranteed. It goes like this with these two: the Cancer man's a real nester. He wants to provide the perfect, comfortable space in which she can uncurl all her erotic energy in his direction. If he has a day off work, he could spend it all in bed with the Capricorn lady by his side and she won't mind, since being physically close to her lover is what life, for her, is all about. And although she'll want to have her fair share of taking the initiative, she's quite happy to cozy up under his warm blanket and be held with the tightness that the Cancer man is famous for. If she wants to try something a little different, it won't rumble him. She could start by making a picnic on the bed since, as far as he's concerned, food and sex go together like sand and sea. He'll be glad to help pack the basket with lots of tasty things to eat and drink, and then he'll provide the dessert for his delicious Capricorn lady.

CAPRICORN WOMAN WITH **LEO MAN**

 In love: The male Lion will prowl around the Capricorn lady, strutting his stuff and showing off to get her hooked on him. And he'll find her a very attractive, trustworthy prey; he can hear her sensuality singing like a finely tuned piano wire that's ready to make beautiful music, while her self-control and physical intensity are like a fascinating barrier just waiting to be broken down. She regards his warmth, refinement, confidence, and raw, creative energy as admirable qualities and she knows that, with her ability to make the most of these traits, the result could be a truly dynamic team. The Capricorn woman is patient and practical; however, the Leo man's ego requires such constant massaging that she may get fed up with always having to serve his needs before she can have her turn. The trade-off, of course, is that he will not begrudge buying her the expensive status symbols that she's so fond of—but she'll probably have words with him about his frivolous spending habits. Is it necessary to buy presents for absolutely everyone? He may not show the appreciation that her satirical wit deserves, particularly if her satire's sometimes directed at him, and she may find his dramatic self-expression a bit too flamboyant for her taste. However, this isn't such an incompatible match as it might appear on the surface.

In bed: Sexy lady, sexy man. And although they express it very differently, their libidos have found their match. Whatever the problems in other areas of the relationship, once these two get into the bedroom, everything else seems petty and unimportant. The Leo man and the Capricorn woman really come into their own between the sheets. Here it's all animal magnetism and raw energy. She'll melt at his touch and get fired up until she erupts with pleasure and he's so uninhibited and openly demonstrative in expressing his sexuality that she feels safe in opening up her own intense, vibrating sensuality. This man can meet her insatiable desire for physical contact so long as she can meet his desire to be admired and worshiped. The maturity and sexual authority that the Capricorn lady brings to this union could have him feeling naughty and possibly even out of his depth, but that's a little game that both could find arousing. She has a deep respect for his masculinity, which means that in bed, she'll treat him like the king he is and, as everyone knows, anyone who treats the male Lion like royalty will get regal treatment in return. However, she might also find him a bit of a handful at times and if it all seems like too much of an effort, she may decide to make her excuses and leave. Either way, they'll know how things are going very quickly.

CAPRICORN WOMAN WITH VIRGO MAN

In love: There's a natural sense of intimacy between a Virgo man and Lady Capricorn. When they go to a party together, though they might split and do their own mingling, they feel the confidence and security of knowing that they'll be back together at the end. In fact, they're so in tune with each other that if one of them needs saving from the bore in the corner, the other will know instinctively and rescue will be just around the corner. With their sense of trust and mutual affection they feel good being together anywhere. The success rate for the Virgo man with the Capricorn woman is very high; the only possible problem might be that they're both so conscientious toward everyone else that they might find it difficult making the time for their own special, intimate moments. Theirs is a very natural love; it just feels so right and is creative in the sense that this is a partnership that has the potential to be much bigger than the sum of its parts. Although it may take the Virgo man a little longer to really commit than the Capricorn woman would like, she's patient and already knows in her bones what he'll realize soon enough—that she has what he wants and needs and that he loves her for having it.

In bed: The sensuality between the Virgo man and Capricorn woman is tangible—it sits like a solid wall of sexual energy simply waiting to be scaled so the heights of erotic pleasure can be attained. Their lovemaking is so intense that it will leave both of them breathless and panting from their exertions. This is very satisfying sex; it's lovemaking for real. They don't need any gadgets, toys, or fantasies but nor will they reject them out of hand because these two feel more playful when wrapped in each other's arms than at any other time. This is what bonds them for life. As a lover, he'll be so attentive to her requirements that she'll respond like never before, which is what he needs to get in touch with the essence of his own sexuality. The Virgo man can take a long time to really explode with passion, so her patience and prowess will pay off. She's the girl who can release him from his need for self-control, and he's the man who'll entice her to reach greater heights than she ever thought possible. And when that happens the earth will shake. It will definitely be worth the effort, though it won't seem like an effort—more like a pleasure. The best part is that these two will never tire of one another.

CAPRICORN WOMAN WITH **LIBRA MAN**

In love: The Libra man and Capricorn lady both have a forward-looking approach to love and life. They have no problem putting in some effort in order to build up a relationship that will provide lasting commitment and scope for their ambitions. She loves his mind and is easily won over by his romantic gestures and she's fascinated that he's able to discuss so many areas of their relationship with her. He, meanwhile, is very impressed by her intensity and willingness to stick to whatever she undertakes, and he finds her cool, calm demeanor very attractive. But he'll drive her mad with his inability to make a decision without endlessly weighing up all the options. That will eventually wear down even the most patient of Capricorns! She'd be delighted if he would simply stop talking about the relationship and start participating in it. They're both natural leaders and need the freedom to rule themselves, so she may even try to take control of his wavering and make the decisions for him, which he'll dislike intensely. He, on the other hand, will have to make space for her occasional serious, brooding moods and shouldn't take them too personally. The tension that could build up between them goes against the ideals that both have of a happy union, so theirs could frequently be an uncomfortable relationship unless there are other factors in their personal charts that make them more compatible.

 In bed: The Libra man just can't seem to make up his mind about whether the mood or timing is right, but with a little encouragement, he'll begin his seduction routine. It may take some time for him to decide whether to do this or that, but the Capricorn woman is patient and when he's done with all his romantic wooing and whispering of sexy scenarios in her ear, they'll both be ready to step things up a notch and to express their feelings physically. Once they get their gear off and get into bed, the tension and sexual energy between them is so tangible that it could be cut with a knife. But it seems a shame that it's such an ordeal getting there. Once they do, though, they'll throw themselves into their sexual satisfaction with a hunger that won't be sated before they've climbed some very dizzy heights and become quite breathless from the exertion. The Capricorn lady will respond to the Libra man's tickling and teasing just as long as he can keep up with her stamina and if she takes the lead, he'll get so turned on by her enthusiasm and apparently insatiable desire for him that he'll immediately stop thinking and dive right in!

CAPRICORN WOMAN WITH **SCORPIO MAN**

In love: This relationship is a fatal attraction but not at all like the movie of the same name—there's no bunny-boiling here! These two individuals both feel a sense of mind-blowing potential when they're in each other's company, so in the early days they'll treat each other with great reverence and respect—and that means that it would be very difficult for them not to fall seriously in love. And it is, indeed, a serious business for both of them for, wherever they are and whatever they are doing, the intensity of their feelings is only just beneath the surface. It consumes them both with a force that's almost scary in its power and will make them lose their heads when they lose their hearts, obliging them to behave in ways that are alien to them. They feel such an unbreakable bond and they give each other such strength that, as a couple, they're invincible. The Scorpio man follows his instincts and he'll sense that, with the Capricorn woman, there's the possibility of a long-lasting love affair, so he'll be on his best behavior. The Capricorn lady, for her part, is always on her best behavior; all she'll want to do is devote herself to him. But all this intensity has the capacity to tear into both of them and hurt really deep down if they're not careful to keep a sense of humor and to do unto the other as they would be done by. However, neither of them will be willing to give up easily on this relationship; it affects them both too deeply— emotionally, mentally, and physically.

In bed: The Scorpio man is on fire with lust for the cool Capricorn lady, but something tells him that he has to contain himself until she gives him the green light. He's not used to waiting or being told what to do, but there's a certain quality about her that tells him she's worth waiting for, so he'd better be serious. Once she gives him the go-ahead, he'll hardly wait for another breath before he'll want to rip her clothes off, take her in his arms, and make love to her until she literally screams with pleasure! She's usually rather good at self-restraint so she may be a little surprised by her own reaction. This is a man who sneaks into erogenous zones that she didn't even know she had. He's a dangerous predator, but that won't stop her from wanting more. Her strong physical desires are more than a match for his passion. Together, the Scorpio man and Capricorn woman won't be able to go any deeper than this level of eroticism. This is something unique and totally exhilarating—sex and sensuality as they've never had it before. It rocks their world and sets a standard that most other lovers would find difficult to attain. It's nothing but pure, passionate pleasure taken to its extreme. When will they ever find the time to sleep?

CAPRICORN WOMAN WITH **SAGITTARIUS MAN**

 In love: The Capricorn woman can't help but be attracted to the imagination and vision of a Sagittarius man. He always has something going on in his mind or in his life, so she'll find tagging along for the ride great fun. Besides, it will give her a chance to gather the raw materials that she needs—some ideological, others of a more practical nature—to build a secure life for the both of them. He loves getting her involved, too, and he's happy in the knowledge that she aspires to a similar quality of life as he does. She has the necessary confidence to allow the roving Sagittarius man to go and find what it is he's looking for, and because he so much appreciates this in her, he always ends up back at her side. They really get on well together because he admires her capable, trustworthy, pragmatic qualities, and she's inspired by his philosophical, optimistic, playful approach to life. And they're especially well suited because, whenever she gets into one of her dark, broody moods, the best thing anyone can do is leave her alone until she works through it, and he's happy to oblige since he is always heading off out anyway. All she need do is make sure that he has his cell phone on him so she can meet up with him when she's ready. The understanding and space that they offer to each other helps build a close, friendly bond. They'll encourage each other to go after what they find important as individuals.

In bed: When the Capricorn woman can actually get hold of her Sagittarius guy and get him to make some time for lovemaking, then she'll discover that this is a very lusty man indeed! She responds well to his touch, since physical contact is the foundation that underpins her sexual awakening, while her intense desire communicates itself to him on a primal, instinctive level and fires him up so much that he just loves romping around the bedroom with her. There's something extremely animalistic about this erotic pairing; he'll track down her sexy scent until his nostrils flare and the wild, untamed aspects of his nature take control of him. The Sagittarius man will be something of a bucking bronco so the Capricorn woman may need all the self-control she can muster, but if anyone can get him to jump over hurdles and set the pace for passionate pleasure, then she can. He may, however, have galloped away before she wakes up in the morning, but hopefully it will just be to fetch the coffee, croissants, and Sunday newspapers. And as she is such a sensually charged lady, she'll always be randy and ready for his return. This sexual duo has a lot to recommend it, but the Capricorn lady could get tired of putting her life on hold while waiting for her Sagittarius man to return. He'll need a very long rein but it could serve more than one purpose; she could use it to whip him into shape once she's pulled him in, but she should never try to tie him down!

CAPRICORN WOMAN WITH **CAPRICORN MAN**

In love: Both of them want the same things in life—status and respect—and both the Capricorn woman and the Capricorn man go about getting these things in the same way. It's also true to say that they both like to have the support of a partner, so why then can it be difficult for a loving relationship to develop between them? Perhaps the reason is that although they're so physical in their expression of love and affection, they also tend to adopt a cool exterior during the initial courting stages and both are reluctant to be the one to break the ice. There could also be an element of competition between them. There's no good reason for it; it just comes naturally when two people love and admire each other so much that they end up comparing themselves to one another. But equally, both will be gunning for the other's success, so together they can make a great team. Once things warm up a bit, they are capable of putting in the time and effort that's needed to develop a truly enlightening, beautiful relationship. Of course, there's a chance that the need of both to be in control of the relationship will cause standoffs and power struggles, but these two pragmatic people soon learn to value what they have and that will be sufficient to make them avoid any subterranean rumbles. Theirs is a good relationship that could be great, and since they are tenacious by nature and prefer to build rather than break down, it's a relationship that has every chance of lasting a long, long time.

In bed: The bedroom is one of the most important geographical locations in the lives of these Capricorn lovers. It's where they can really reach the heights of the relationship, where clashing egos melt away, and where they can fully express their drive to experience one another in the flesh. Both crave the sensuality of close physical contact and they have a powerful hunger for sex. There's a kind of familiarity between them even before they take all their clothes off, but that doesn't make it any less exciting. It's just that, for them, there's no uncomfortable guessing needed so they can get on with the business of pleasuring one another and feeling the incredibly intense vibes that bounce between them. Because everything will be equal between them on all levels, there's no limit to the gratification they can give and receive, though it might take them a while to get going as they both like to build the sexual excitement gradually before attempting a rousing crescendo. They'll be wrapped together in passionate embrace all night long, their patient self-control and intense eroticism creating a sublime friction that has them quaking long before the dawn chorus becomes their lullaby. It's a stamina thing, and the only competition between them will be to see who can last the longest. There might be a little tussling for authority, but since giving pleasure is as important to them as receiving it, they both usually get their fair share of each.

CAPRICORN WOMAN WITH **AQUARIUS MAN**

 In love: On a mental level, the Aquarius man is a truly stimulating partner for the Capricorn woman and on a spiritual level they can really connect. But on the physical and emotional levels, she could very well scare the hell out of Mr. Aquarius. Her type of intensity makes him feel obliged to live up to her high expectations and even if it's all only in his mind, he can find it very restricting, particularly when he's in a gregarious, lighthearted mood. He doesn't bow to authority and prefers to break the rules rather than make them, while she'll never know whether she's coming or going and she can't look to him for answers because he has no idea what she's talking about. However, if the aloof Mr. Aquarius and the cool Ms. Capricorn do develop a fondness for each other, it will be a profound and strong one. Without him even realizing it, she'll help tame his wayward drift—though she'll never change him. He'd never agree to that! He does have a genuinely loyal streak and will devote his heart, at least, to her, while she'll give him some tolerance, which is the final ingredient that's needed for a very perfect, palpable romantic mix. They'll never get bored when they're talking about the important, earth-shattering subjects they find of interest, and when they're joking and playing around together, they really make a connection, since both find life and themselves a little absurd. From there on, love can crystallize into something quite beautiful and long-lived.

In bed: What an intriguing lover this guy is. One minute he can't get enough of his lovely Capricorn lady, the next he's on automatic pilot, his mind is way out there, and she might as well be with a dummy! But the Aquarius man can be an inventive, original lover so she'll never be bored even though she won't always recognize the man who's lying next to her in bed. This could be exciting or confusing, depending on her mood. He'll soon realize how important foreplay is to the Capricorn woman, and how much time he needs to invest in stoking up her erotic passions, but this is something he can do very well, particularly when he's getting the right response. But just when he's built her up to a crackling electrical storm of pleasure, he could get distracted, flip the switch, and short-circuit, and then it will be Ms. Capricorn's turn to blow a fuse. Their differences could make the lovemaking a little unpredictable, and the Capricorn woman prefers to know what's going to happen next, but the Aquarius man will quite naturally raise her temperature so, for better or for worse, she'll definitely get hot. What they do have in common will be enough to keep them together. It's hardly ever the same each time they bump into one another, so instead of things grinding to a halt, variety will be the spice of their sexual life.

CAPRICORN WOMAN WITH **PISCES MAN**

 In love: The Capricorn woman will really fall for the dreamy, romantic Pisces guy. She's a closet romantic herself, and he nudges her in just the right way to bring it all tumbling out into the open. He encourages her to share her feelings with him and talk about emotional issues, which is something she finds quite unique in a man. In return, she will listen to him when he wants to say how he feels, for she can easily contain the vast well of emotion that he has to express. His imagination and sensitivity capture her heart, providing her with a much-needed sense of relaxation while still giving the feeling of purpose that will build a close and loving bond between them. He is easily addicted to her expressive sensuality and is very impressed by her wisdom and the hard-earned symbols of her success. Both of them have such lofty ideals and such breadth of understanding that it's fantastic for them to have found someone with whom they can share their thoughts. They could get so wound up in each other, however, that other important people and tasks in their lives get left behind, which, in the long run, will freak out the Capricorn woman and not be healthy for the Pisces man. Their love does have such potential for development that it will keep them both happy for many years. It could surely be the most beautiful and romantic relationship the Capricorn woman will ever have, and the most deeply secure, supportive, and profound relationship of the Pisces man.

In bed: For all his shyness and sensitivity, Mr. Pisces is more than a match for the insatiable physical appetites of Ms. Capricorn. There's a sense of relief when these two come together and release their tension. Although, in their own way, both can be shy, when they get together they are eager to reveal themselves to one another, for there's an unspoken feeling of love and acceptance between them. Their inhibitions are stripped away as they remove each item of clothing. He wants to show himself in his full glory and lose himself completely in her, and she'll be keen and very welcoming. She might be very much in control of herself with other lovers, but this guy makes it possible for her to truly surrender and be carried away on waves of passion. If she's hooked on this Fish, she definitely won't want to throw him back, and once he's seen who's caught him, he won't let her! She has exactly what this man has been looking for in a lover—an intense sensuality that rocks the very foundations of his desire. Her sexuality is solid and secure but if there are any cracks, he'll find them and fill them with his own brand of sensuality so that they both feel complete.

THE **CAPRICORN MAN** IN LOVE

The Capricorn man isn't someone who immediately stands out in a crowd. He doesn't make a lot of noise or gesture wildly, so if a lady is scanning around on the lookout for a desirable date, she could easily miss him. His appearance is rather straight, unemotional, and sober, although there's a wealth of treasures hidden inside him that aren't always so easy to understand. Few people manage to get really close to Capricorn men because they tend to keep themselves to themselves and expect others to do the same. They are reserved and watchful, yet they know to strike when the iron is hot. They have an acute understanding of their environment and when they feel moved to take action, they don't hang around.

The Capricorn man will have spotted that lady who's looking around the room for her Mr. Right long before she sets eyes on him. In fact, if he senses something good, he won't hesitate to move right over to where she's standing, strike up a conversation, and immediately start wooing her. He might seem a little standoffish, but he's not one to hesitate when an opportunity presents itself. Once the Goat takes someone into his life, then that someone will enjoy his steadfast loyalty and a helping hand whenever it's needed. The Capricorn man can be very self-sacrificing and would sooner give the shirt off his back than see someone suffer. That side of him should never be underestimated; it can show itself in several ways. Firstly, there's the workaholic, who wants the best for his wife and family. Then there's the unhappy lover, who'd put up with anything to keep the relationship going. He's determinedly staunch and will endure the most difficult and undesirable situations in order to attain his wishes. The problem with this, however, is that eventually he'll want some kind of recompense for having worn his hair shirt; he'll be looking for demonstrative love, loyalty, and devotion to match his, but unfortunately, life isn't always so accommodating. What the Capricorn man really wants and needs is a very physical expression of love; he won't be satisfied with displays of love that are purely emotional or intellectual.

The lady who offers this very deserving man the physical presence, dedication, love, and support that he appreciates will, in return, receive all the stability and faithfulness she could want, plus romantic gestures, sensual satisfaction, and all the perks of his job, including prestige and material comfort. There's one little hitch, though, and that is that he can be something of a control freak, a characteristic that's as evident in his love life as it is everywhere else. He seeks a deep, intense, spiritual connection to the lover he commits to, and his earthy sexuality is one way he tries to achieve it. What more could a woman want? He knows how to treat her well!

CAPRICORN MAN WITH **ARIES WOMAN**

In love: If she is an Aries woman of a more serious persuasion, the Capricorn man will appeal to her sense of purpose and determination. Likewise, if he's the type of Goat that enjoys the occasional nudge up the mountain, he'll be very attracted by the pushy lady Ram. Both are ambitious and self-reliant, and at best, this relationship could get them where they want to go that little bit faster. However, this is unlikely to be a sumptuously romantic pairing. It's a love that needs time to mature because Capricorns are not known for their impulsive actions and, unfortunately, the Aries woman doesn't like to wait around. She knows her feelings immediately and won't take kindly to his testing each stage of the relationship to make sure it's safe to move on to the next step. She expects him to open his heart as readily as she does, but the Capricorn man is just not like that. His loyalty needs to be earned. The Capricorn man could use an Aries woman to help him to loosen up and try being spontaneous rather than planning everything, while she needs him to remind her to look before she leaps. As both are Cardinal signs, they could clash when each thinks he's right, but if they can agree to agree before disagreeing, or at least agree to disagree, they could have something very special going between them. This is not the most comfortable of relationships and it will require work, but if they're both willing to meet halfway, it could be very rewarding.

In bed: When it comes to sex, the Capricorn man is very physical and highly composed. He could move the earth for any deserving female. He's the master of self-control and discipline yet he's not one to risk a fleeting passion so the Aries woman will have to wait for him to initiate the process. There it is again! That "waiting" thing. But the Aries woman would be well advised to wait for this guy. The male Goat's passion is so coiled up inside him that once he lets go, one of the few people that could handle the intensity of his sensual ardor is an Aries. And boy will she handle him! He'll be incredibly turned on by her enthusiastic expressions of love and her sense of adventure will delight his lingering libido. But getting to this stage of the relationship might take longer than the Aries lady is willing to wait. If she is aware of what she might be missing if she doesn't wait for him, it might still work out because he offers not just a promise of satisfaction. She'll be quaking after all his deliberations. And he'll be moved, too, so the rhythm between them becomes self-perpetuating, and once they get going, there will be no stopping them!

CAPRICORN mAN WiTH **TAURUS WOmAN**

In love: Earthy, passionate, physical, and ambitious. These two lovers are on the same level and, what is more, they both want to go higher. The Taurus woman and Capricorn man understand each other superbly well, and the result is mutual trust and respect. What better foundation could there be for a long and lasting love? Since they're both totally absorbed in one another's aspirations, each is able to bring out the best in the other. Between them they have a mutual support system going. The sensuous Taurus lady is everything the Capricorn man could ever want in a woman. She's practical, sensible, and deliciously romantic. She thrills to his touch and offers him an abundance of affection. The Capricorn man is trustworthy and steady, serious when necessary, yet with a wonderfully ironic sense of humor that really tickles her fancy—all of which are major attractions for the Taurus woman. This is not a love that could ever be threatened by outside influences, no matter how tempting, so he's never going to feel vulnerable or she jealous. The Capricorn man might, at times, display a coolness that seems almost impenetrable, but her natural warmth and consistent tenderness will eventually break down any barriers. Their material aims are alike: both choose quality over quantity any day, so squabbles over money are non-existent. Because these two have such similar ideals, they are able to sense the divine spark in one another and their love could truly carry them into heaven.

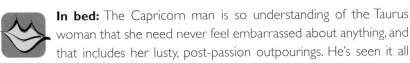 **In bed:** The Capricorn man is so understanding of the Taurus woman that she need never feel embarrassed about anything, and that includes her lusty, post-passion outpourings. He's seen it all before and, because he's so enamored of the Lady Bull, will gladly lap up everything she offers. His practicality means he has a waste-not want-not attitude! Bedroom manners? The Capricorn man is the perfect gentleman to his Taurus woman; he always says, "After you, m'lady," to which she always

accedes with quivering grace. From the outside, this couple might look like Mr. and Mrs. Conventional, but once they're alone, they're anything but. There's a deliciously naughty side to their relationship, with him as a randy Goat and she enjoying the role of wood-nymph dancing to his pan-pipes. They love a pastoral frolic around the bedroom together. The intensity of their combined sexual energy is earth-shattering and they'll make the most of it. The only problem that these two have to tackle is, with all their worldly ambitions and activities, when do they ever find enough time to indulge their sensual appetites? What they always need to remember is that their powerful sexy bond is the glue holding their relationship together.

CAPRICORN MAN WITH GEMINI WOMAN

In love: The Capricorn man is an old soul so if the Gemini girl is into father figures, there's great scope for her here. He could look after her for life and takes the responsibility of caring for fragile little creatures very seriously. That's alright with her up to a point, but she's not as fragile as all that and needs him to be a playmate at least some of the time. She won't like being scolded like a child when all she wants to do is indulge in a bit of frivolous fun. If she's got a masochistic streak, then she'll have met her match. He's heavy, intense, and brooding; she's lighthearted, cheerful, and flirtatious. That isn't to say that they're entirely incompatible. Everyone has their moments and if these are coordinated, they could hit it off. If they both get most of their mental stimulus outside of the relationship, from work, family, and friends, they could find the nest they create together rather refreshing. And there are instances when their dissimilarities are a good thing, for instance when it comes to humor. The Gemini girl is quick and witty enough to grasp his sense of irony and satire and bounce it straight back, to the delight of both. Her youthful zest enlivens his low-key, somber habits, but some attempts to lighten him up, particularly when he is under the shadow of a cold, dark mood, will just irritate him and in response he'll put a chill around her heart that will have her picking icicles off for weeks.

In bed: The old soul and the young at heart can be an exciting combination when they get together between the sheets. When the man in her bed is a stuffy, self-controlled Capricorn, she relishes the challenge to intrigue and seduce him. Not that it takes much of an effort; he's really into physical pursuits, and sex is his favorite. He knows exactly how to bring his Gemini lady to an ecstatic high, and she will never tire of the way he unflaggingly indulges her. Nothing brings out the kid in a Goat quite like the prospect of sexual tomfoolery. She may have to warm her hands in order to arouse his deeper passions, and this could take longer than she's used to, but the more time he can spend stringing out the sexual experience, the better it is as far as he's concerned. For him, making love is a serious business, but he's renowned for his stamina, so the Gemini girl should prepare herself for a long, long night. Once he carries her to his peak, rest assured there's no free-fall drop. He'll hold on tight and take her down the scenic route.

CAPRICORN MAN WITH **CANCER WOMAN**

In love: The Cancer woman and the Capricorn man could easily grow old together, though they may do it before they reach 30! These are opposite signs of the zodiac, so they'll attract one another like magnets then settle in for the long haul. When they are together, they are one, like the yin-yang symbol—opposites that together create the perfect union. There's a degree of comfort and mutual approval between them that makes this link very close, and everything seems so natural between them. Both are dynastically-minded people who will unconsciously get one another's scent and instantly decide that the other has what's needed to continue the family line. There's no doubt there's a big love between them. It's as if they have been looking for one another their whole lives. When they finally meet there's a sense of completion that will be continued on into the next phase of their journey together. Since they are working toward the same goals, they share a feeling of security and joint purpose that make this relationship as easy as riding a tandem bike. The Capricorn man is a serious lover who'll never leave his lady guessing as to his devotion. Even when he's at his most practical and purposeful, she'll know that it's because he wants to take the world onto his shoulders and the weight off hers. He'll love the way she fusses over him, so her caring and protective instincts couldn't find a better object. These two will be riding off into the sunset together.

In bed: Procreation is recreation when it comes to the Cancer woman and Capricorn man. They won't be able to leave each other alone until they can hear the sound of tiny pattering feet around their home. Okay, well, they can wait, but both feel instinctively that this is their objective when they're together. But don't worry. It doesn't end when their kids are grown, for the love between them is everlasting. Now back to basics. These two have an instinct for getting down and dirty with one another. The Capricorn man can be gentle yet penetrating, so she'll soon happily slip out of her shell and into something more comfortable—like his bed. He'll rise to the occasion and satisfy all her needs, yet he possesses the sensitivity to know when she only wants a cuddle. Her little sideways seduction movements will intrigue and entice him, but he won't miss a trick when it comes to the possibility of being with her in an intensely intimate, magical clinch. They'll keep each other forever limber and lithe for their bedroom antics. He'll go on and on, because the delicate yet exciting sensual responses of his Cancer woman will urge him on to higher levels of passion. She'll completely lose track of time when they're together, but may soon decide that early nights are the only answer to her continual lack of sleep.

CAPRICORN MAN WITH **LEO WOMAN**

In love: What the Leo lady loves and respects about the Capricorn guy is the fact that he's so responsible. She also has a strong sense of responsibility and two people with such dependable characters make for one successful couple. They will love each other, if for nothing else than the level of productivity that they achieve together. The Capricorn man loves that the Leo woman adds a touch of danger and excitement to his life. She does what he would never consider doing; he loves watching her and respects her for being gutsy and courageous. She'll admire his endless ambition, especially for where it takes them as a couple. There will be times when he sees her flamboyance as too showy and her extravagance as a waste, just as she sometimes wishes he weren't so cautious and would be prepared to take a risk now and then. She's such a naturally positive person, gregarious, alive, and with such a sense of fun, that it will be hard for her to indulge his occasional black, brooding moods. He, on the other hand, won't appreciate her attempts to jolly him out of those moods; he knows that they pass in their own good time. Although these two are elementally different, both rate status and prestige, so give them some development time together and they'll really hit it off.

In bed: It may take some time for the Leo woman to warm up to the deceptively cold Capricorn man, but she's persistent and he's very patient. It will be well worth the wait! She is passionate, warm, and embracing—the perfect woman to light his fire, and once she does, she'll find his insatiable sexual appetite decidedly devilish. This is one very physical and seriously sensual man. He knows how to set the stage with soft candlelight and incense so his lovely Lioness can perform for him. Seeing his controlled disposition, she'll never guess what he's capable of and she'll be pleasantly surprised by his unimaginably deep, sensuous nature. There's not a lot of room for play, however, for he's pretty serious. Satirical humor is his style but if she's willing, he'd be delighted by the Leo lady who can play the part of a dark temptress. Her unbound fiery passion has an extraordinary effect on him, releasing all his powerful emotions and animal hunger, and when he relinquishes control, they could both be in for a bit of a surprise.

CAPRICORN MAN WITH VIRGO WOMAN

In love: The ambitious, aspiring, expressive Goat couldn't do better than to have a Virgo woman by his side. He admires the way her clear-thinking brain works and the fact that she is capable and self-reliant, but what he really loves is her quiet allure and feminine charms. She'll enjoy helping her upwardly mobile Capricorn man to reach the goals he sets himself because he'll share every one of his achievements completely with her. She can see the detail that needs to be attended to along the way, while he focuses his attention on getting to the top. This is a mutually encouraging, wonderfully supportive partnership, and they find it really easy to love one another. Their connection goes beyond the creation of a luxurious life filled with material things and status symbols, though they often both find that a very attractive by-product. These two are true soul mates; as soon as they meet, they feel spiritually at home. It's not something that they can put into words; it's just a feeling, a sense of a special compatibility between them. As well as being more interested in expanding their minds than their bank balances, they share a wickedly ironic sense of humor and an appreciation of the ridiculous. They find that, with each other more than with any other person, they can be playfully affectionate or seriously funny as the mood takes them. But best of all, when a loving, romantic mood washes over them, they can completely immerse themselves in one another.

 In bed: When Pan takes out his pipe, the Virgin dances to the tune, and the longer she dances, the more of a frenzy she'll find herself in. The Capricorn man has what it takes to get that white-hot fire burning inside the Virgo woman, and he's got the stamina to stoke the flames for hours. His intensely coiled sexuality and the steady rhythm of his sensuality will have her whirling like a dervish and will elicit unexpected responses, while no man could appreciate her skillful touch more than he does. This complete sense of physical connection is something he's longed to feel; it allows him to abandon his self-control, yet be himself and be totally self-indulgent. But this isn't about trying out new techniques or constantly assessing each other's performance; it's a real partnership whose growing intimacy is founded on a deep mutual respect that doesn't necessarily depend on sexual prowess. It's about an appreciation of the other's gender—her gorgeous femininity, and his beautiful masculinity. That's what turns them on from the depths of their souls. When they make love, they see the innate beauty in one another as in the universe. This is as near divinity as it gets for two Earth signs. Yet they're both so realistic about their mutual attraction and desire for each other that they just know that they'll end up in bed together.

CAPRICORN MAN WiTH **LiBRA WOMAN**

In love: In many ways, the Libra woman and the Capricorn man were made for each other. Given time, the things that they have in common will help them achieve a very comfortable lifestyle. Both are ambitious and, to some extent, they share the same refinement of taste and the same standards. However, if they're not careful about the things that they don't agree on, this relationship could result in tension and discomfort for them both. The Capricorn man finds the lovely Libra lady very attractive; he appreciates her mind just as much as he appreciates the attention that she pays to her appearance. He'll want to capture her and pin her down, but is it ever possible to pin down a delicate butterfly without doing her some damage? The Libra woman wants to be in a committed relationship, one where she can talk about and share the ideals and fantasies that her man has for the two of them. She'll love his sense of responsibility and the stability he offers her but at times, she might find him too down-to-earth to be a dreamer and this could be a real downer to her lightheartedness. Of course, the Caprircorn man does have dreams, big dreams, but he's much too coolly practical ever to express them out loud until he's fairly certain that achieving them is well within his grasp. Unfortunately, that could be too late for her. However, there is a powerful energy when these two are together; it's both exciting and a little scary. Their love won't flow easily but it will certainly be intense.

In bed: It has to be said that the sensual Capricorn man is a really randy Goat! He wants the Libra lady and she knows it! He won't be satisfied with fantasy foreplay—flirty, teasing conversations or chasing her around the bedroom to build up her excitement levels. He needs physical contact, and lots of it! It's always good when they get going but she shouldn't expect him to wait for her to be in the mood. She needs to be able to supply sex on demand—and he'll be demanding it all the time! The Capricorn man simply isn't capable of watching her move gracefully across the room without having a powerful physical reaction, but who would ever have guessed it from his sober-looking exterior? Well, Lady Libra will know it by the way he devours her with his eyes. They may be out to dinner, for example, and he'll suddenly get the urge. He only has to give her one look and she'll not only be blushing, she'll be squirming with eagerness. But they'll have to contain themselves until they get home because the public restrooms won't provide either of them with the atmosphere they need! And that's when the randy Goat really needs to watch his step because, although she was all for it in the restaurant, by the time they get home her sexual scales may have tipped slightly out of balance. If he charges her into the bedroom before he's got her libido going again, then neither of them will get the satisfaction that they crave.

CAPRICORN MAN WITH SCORPIO WOMAN

In love: A Scorpio woman will simply adore the emotional complexity of the Capricorn man. He's like an endless puzzle that she can explore, and because he's built his character on such firm foundations, she'll feel safe and secure in the expression of his love. He's the solid earth that can contain her watery depth of emotion. These two are good for one another; in many ways they're made for each other and they have a naturally strong affinity for one another. Both possess a kind of profound wisdom that each understands and needs in a partner, and they also share a dark sense of humor that brings out their wicked side. He aspires to great things and she could be the woman who helps him to achieve them, or even vice versa. There's a touch of the tormented soul about this man, but he never feels sorry for himself and that simply makes her love him even more. He, on the other hand, will treasure her femininity, strength, and commitment. He has no problem with her need to delve into the darker aspects of her own psyche and his. Indeed, he encourages her because he, too, longs for the creative outlet that her intensity, deep emotions, and eroticism bring to their relationship. If a few aspects of his character are destroyed in the process then, as far as he's concerned, they weren't worth having in the first place. These two are able to make sacrifices for one another without either demanding that they do, and both are equally willing to make this partnership last.

In bed: This is sexual heaven for the Scorpio lady; her Capricorn man is earthy, horny, and totally addicted to his sensual pleasures. She'll never have to question his love; she really turns him on and he can't help but make it obvious to her every day and in a very physical way. Whether it's the first embrace of the morning or the last little hug at night, she'll know it alright. There's always a subtle erotic hint present in her aura and it simply seems to envelop them both when they're together, raising their sexual awareness imperceptibly, but always leaving them ready and willing to get it on in an instant. Her predatory, penetrating gaze seduces him completely and he simply can't wait to return the compliment. It delights the Scorpio woman that he's so insatiably hungry for all the delicious sexual delicacies she has to offer. One touch leads to a stroke, which leads to a caress, and that takes them all the way down that slippery slope again and again. He could be the only man who has what it takes to absorb the entire ocean of her passions, or at least it seems that way. She could throw the whole weight of her intense eroticism, as well as her body, against him and he'd emerge breathless but eager for more.

CAPRICORN MAN WITH **SAGITTARIUS WOMAN**

In love: A very deep bond can develop between the Sagittarius woman and the Capricorn man. He's very attracted to her warmth, optimism, and willingness to live life to the full and she has an interesting way of looking at the world, which he finds to be both inspiring and enlightening. She, for her part, will be extremely susceptible to his ironic sense of humor, his intense physical energy, and his natural wisdom concerning both the world as a whole and his personal life. These two can do amazing things together because they both aspire to something higher— a spiritual and creative life. She'll feed him the ideas and wild dreams and show him their potential, and he'll make them reality. When they are together, their lives can be very productive, creative, and fulfilling, with the love between them arising from their respect for and admiration of one another. The relationship might not live up to Lady Sagittarius's ideal of romance and may not offer her the freedom to roam about as she pleases, but it is certainly the next best thing. The Capricorn man will have to devote a certain amount of his energy toward taming her, but that will help to keep the energy flowing between them. If she needs an occasional night out or a weekend away with the girls, then he's pragmatic enough not to stop her, but as soon as she's home, she'd better be prepared to be wooed by a moody man because the lack of physical contact will have left him feeling a bit depressed.

In bed: The horny Goat really wants to get down and get sexy— and all the time. He's not fussy about where or when they do it, and neither is she, so long as they get on with it! The Capricorn man has a tendency to behave a bit as though he were a teacher, so he can't help but want to teach his Sagittarius lady his new dimension to lovemaking, and she makes a very attentive student. But things aren't all one-sided; she'll show him a thing or two about red-hot passion. She'll be so mad with anticipation that the Capricorn man will simply have to follow her lead. That's just what she wants but will he mind that she's managed to gain control? Can he stop her? Maybe not, but he'll do his best to get into the driving seat. Sometimes their erotic adventures will give them a long leisurely ride at a comfortable pace, allowing them to take in all the subtleties as they go. Other times it will be a hilariously bumpy, boisterous, fun-filled jaunt, over rough-and-tumble territory. But mostly it will seem like a thrillingly paced grand prix; there'll be very few pit stops, and they'll be sweating from exertion and completely exhausted as they race across the finish line. And then they'll have the popping corks and spurting champagne to enjoy as well. This is a winning combination in the bedroom at least, if nowhere else.

CAPRICORN MAN WITH **CAPRICORN WOMAN**

See pages 69–71.

CAPRICORN MAN WITH **AQUARIUS WOMAN**

 In love: Both will be surprised by the unusually powerful attraction that exists between them. The Aquarius woman has the ability to bring out the irresponsible child lying buried deep within the Capricorn man, and he loves her for it. His searching soul and intense need to make sense of this senseless world easily seduce her insatiable, inquiring mind. Both have a broad vision, and their inexhaustibly long conversations that take place into the wee hours of the night have a wonderful way of turning fantasy into reality. If they never slept, they'd probably solve all the problems of the world in one extended sitting, but they'd always be interrupted by the need to delve deeply into each other's physicality. However, the Aquarius girl may sometimes find it difficult to meet his demands for a more intense expression of love, which doesn't come easily to her. She'll suppress her emotional reactions until she can express them verbally. At times, she'll feel the urge to rebel against his stern traditionalism and will demonstrate her love in such an original way that he either won't get it at all or won't like it. He may think that by providing her with material comfort and physical attention he has the right to some control over her life, but she's too independent to allow that. At the end of it all, both are realistic enough to recognize that their differences could enhance their relationship, but they'll also know whether, in this case, there are simply too many differences for it to succeed.

In bed: He's sexy, insatiable, and intense. The Capricorn man is a horny old Goat no matter what his age, and for the experimental Aquarius woman that's a real turn-on. She'll certainly want to try him on for size and to try out some of her own new tricks and turns, too. She'll have a bit of a surprise with this randy Goat, though, because until she gets naked with him, his sober appearance won't give away his deep eroticism. He'll be right in there with her, and he's got the stamina and patience to put up with her endless experimentation. Thankfully, she's a quick study and because he likes all forms of physical loving, even her more wacky ideas will simply fill him with amusement and a willingness to indulge her. But where she can get off on sexual fantasy, his needs are all down and dirty. When they're not together, this guy won't be satisfied by late-night phone sex; he wants her there next to him. If she ever planned to turn him on this way, then she should think again, because the moment she hangs up the phone, he'll be grabbing his address book and reaching for his coat to go in search of a flesh-and-blood lover. When their moods coincide then the peaks of pleasure they can reach are limitless, but when they don't, it all feels like a lead balloon. This coupling is sometimes so right and sometimes so not. Either way, they'll both be in for an unforgettable ride.

CAPRICORN MAN WITH **PISCES WOMAN**

 In love: Love grows steadily deeper, more enriching, and more intimate when Mr. Goat and Lady Fish spend time together. She can trust him with her heart and soul, for he's as steady as a rock and easy to cling to when she starts riding the waves of emotion. He longs to immerse himself in her and feel her soft, sensitive feelings washing all over him. In the Capricorn man, the Pisces lady has found the guy who can turn her dreams and fantasies into both practical and sensual reality. A strong sense of fulfillment accompanies this relationship; she needs his anchor and he needs taking out of himself, which she can do so well. She has a feminine allure that is highly intoxicating and seductive to this stern, self-contained man, for he secretly longs to feel total, abandoned love and he senses that this is the woman to help him do it. He can be a touch rigid and pedantic, which can put a strain on her more imaginative, dreamy nature, but she accepts and understands his reasons. He would be an especially wonderful, supportive partner for the Pisces woman with career ambitions because he'd really get involved and offer solid, practical help. The more time they spend together, the better this relationship gets. Their love could go on forever, and then for a little while longer.

In bed: Happiness wells up inside him and comes tumbling out when these two sensual lovers make it together. It's quite a powerful thing to be able to do that to a man and it's down to the perfect sexual blend that exists between Mr. Capricorn and Ms. Pisces. She soothes him with her soft caresses and with the way she totally surrenders her body to his masterful application of erotic pleasure. She feels completely embraced and fulfilled by his masculinity, and thoroughly enjoys the sensation of his tightly coiled sexual intensity wrestling with his incredible self-control. She enjoys it so much that she won't need to drift off into the nether realms of her imagination because he'll keep her fascinated and involved right to the point where he loses his battle. Reality is far more beautiful when she's with him. He's sexually insatiable and a little controlling, so if she feels like acting the sex slave, all she has to do is throw herself into the role and walk around the place naked, pandering to his every need—

and then who really has the power? With the right combination of shy looks and wiggling hips she could soon have him following her around like a puppy dog. These two adore one another and sex in the most delicious, delectable positions possible brings them both to the point of worship. It's such an intoxicating cocktail of sensuality and eroticism that they'll be licking their lips in order to savor every last drop.